MIDDLE RAGES

MIDDLE RAGES

WHY THE BATTLE FOR MEDIEVAL STUDIES MATTERS TO AMERICA

MILO YIANNOPOULOS

DANGEROUS BOOKS

Middle Rages
Why The Battle For Medieval Studies Matters To America

Milo Yiannopoulos

Published by Dangerous Books
Second Edition
First published July 2018 on dangerous.com

Cover Design: Milo Yiannopoulos

CONTENTS

TO JOHN

Love is weal and love is woe, in gladness can maintain us;
Love is life and love is death, and love can well sustain us.

—Anonymous, 13th Century England

For if a priest be foul, on whom we trust,
No wonder is a common man should rust

—Geoffrey Chaucer, *The Canterbury Tales*

FOREWORD

To any objective observer of higher education over the last thirty or so years, it is now clear that the multiculturalist project announced in pleasing, benign terms of "diversity" and "opening up the canon" and "recovering lost voices" was no such thing. Multiculturalists spoke warmly of honoring the Other and welcoming historically-disadvantaged groups, but now that the diversiphiles have changed the curriculum for good and altered hiring practices—for instance, by adding to job interviews litmus-test questions such as, "How will you enhance diversity at our school after we hire you?"—they aren't happy and they aren't satisfied.

No, the most fervent among them, though they have ample cause for self-congratulation, don't feel like they have accomplished very much, and they certainly have no gratitude for what they have achieved. Instead, they're bitter and vindictive. In their mouths, the old call for inclusion has turned into vigilant practices of exclusion. The affirmative promises of a richer, fuller, more accurate understanding of the past and its greatnesses have given way to scapegoating, victimology, and *ressentiment*.

The strange case of Professor Rachel Fulton Brown of the University of Chicago is an exemplary drama. Here we have several common features of academic decay: the politicization of a scholarly field, the arousal of tribal resentments, allegations of white supremacy, a victim of color, a white perpetrator, a protest letter with many, many signatures, and a compliant media. Each one of those elements is open to an identitarian reading—which would be mistaken in every line. But how can one correct it when the entire field, academia in general, and the media reporting on it share the bias?

That's why this little book by Milo Yiannopoulos is a necessary read. We hear endless generalizations about identity politics in academia, and those generalizations largely hold true. What we need now, however, are specific, detailed accounts of how identity politics actually unfold in particular times and places—the facts, the contexts, the personnel. If you don't work inside the system, you can't easily comprehend the peculiar mores and protocols of academic life, not to mention the sometimes daffy and always tense institutional psychology that goes with them.

Middle Rages is exactly the kind of thick description that reveals the perverse group dynamic and anti-intellectual ossification into which the humanities have deteriorated. I will not disclose its conclusions—that would kill the joy of reading Milo's crisp narration—but be it said that the truth comes forth in full display and persuasively contradicts popular renditions in the education press of the controversy. Fifteen hundred academics signed a letter denouncing Professor Brown, but not because she harassed an outspoken medievalist of color. That crime was a fabrication. Rather, they signed the letter because they wanted to signal their virtue, because they wanted their colleagues to think well of them, or because they wanted to ease for a moment their liberal guilt.

How this ludicrous outcome happened, and how it has continued to play out, and why identity politics should have chosen so arcane a theater as Medieval Studies—those are questions to be answered only after the facts are described and the parties faithfully profiled. The story Milo tells will lead readers well past leftist myths and color mainstream coverage of academic disputes. If we want honesty and reality in higher education, if we wish to see how those goods have been distorted by identity politics and political correctness, this book is essential.

Prof. Mark Bauerlein
Emory University

PROLOGUE

Standing at five feet five inches and weighing barely 130 pounds—"Just say size eight," she tells me during fact-checking—Professor Rachel Fulton Brown doesn't look like the dangerous woman her critics describe. But she has become used to reading outlandish descriptions of herself since June 2015, when she published a blog post titled "Three Cheers For White Men," effectively dropping a barrel of gunpowder into a burgeoning internecine war within Medieval Studies.

Three years and hundreds of blog posts later, the tenured University of Chicago history professor is being casually referred to as a "fascist" at medievalist conferences, accused of inciting physical violence and rape against her peers, and avoided like a strumpet with bubonic plague. She has been called a "Nazi cunt" on Twitter and was even called out for bad language by Mark Zuckerberg's sister, Donna.

Fulton Brown's blog post wasn't, as her critics claim, a veiled defense of white nationalism, or anything like it. She was responding playfully to the "dead white male" trope in academia, gently pointing out that the wicked Caucasian dudes of social justice folklore were responsible for, among other things, the development of chivalry, consensual marriage and, to some extent, the success of feminism itself. But her post went down like a cup of cold sick anyway. Dozens, later hundreds, of Fulton Brown's colleagues declared war on her, incensed by her refusal to back down and apologize—and by the fact that she had blogged approvingly, a number of times, about a rising star in conservative media who was causing eruptions on campuses with his scathing commentary about the finger-wagging campus Left.

Fulton Brown was taken to task for refusing to acknowledge the problematic "whiteness" of her field and her responsibility as a Medieval Studies professor to "do something about it." But a dozen senior professors interviewed for this story say something very specific and different is happening: an attempt to inject into the study of the Middle Ages the same far-Left identity politicking that has done so much damage to liberal arts departments.

In the course of writing this story, I have interviewed scholars, journalists and authors, many of whom privately confided that Medieval Studies needed a Rachel Fulton Brown to draw a line in the sand, because, for the past half-decade, gender warriors and race scholars with axes to grind have been on a mission to change the field irreversibly. Sympathetic, but hitherto silent, colleagues say the attempt to destroy Fulton Brown is part of a larger invasion into the discipline by activist academics, who see their role as arbiters of moral taste, determined to rid the field of infidels who refuse to bow to social justice.

You've read stories before about academics at war over free speech with their own institutions. This is different. It's the story of a professor who has taken on her entire academic field, with no backing whatsoever from the University of Chicago, an institution that prides itself on its commitment to free speech and academic freedom. What's more, the crazy bitch might even win.

I

INQUISITION

It started gently, the waters tested with light mockery. But it quickly descended into an almost unprecedented attempt at academic sororicide. Fulton Brown, who maintains an enthusiastic online presence, was first ridiculed by snooty colleagues in academia for engaging with "random laypersons" through her blog, *Fencing Bear at Prayer*, and her Facebook page, as though speaking to the public or explaining oneself in plain English was beneath the dignity of a serious historian.

Fulton Brown appeared unfazed by this: within a week or two of the criticism appearing online, she was distributing "RANDOM LAYPERSON" t-shirts and mugs to readers of her blog. She is a product of Middle America's tradition of educating girls, hailing from a four-generation long line of women who attended college in Arkansas, Missouri and Texas, and she says that's the reason she feels an obligation to engage with regular folk outside the academy.

But then came the sinister name-calling, the associations with racism, and the repeated, direct assaults on her credentials and her standing in the field. Karl Steel, a medievalist at the City University of New York, remarked on Twitter that Fulton Brown probably wasn't doing much peer reviewing any more, gloating about imagined damage done to her career by reckless allegations that he himself had helped to spread that Fulton Brown was consorting with "white nationalists," and was condemned by association, according to tweets and emails seen by this author. Steel had been the one to christen her readers "random laypersons." He did not respond to a request for comment.

With every fresh round of allegations, Fulton Brown published a light-hearted rebuttal on *Fencing Bear At Prayer*, drenched in medieval references and good-natured humor. Months went by, and it wasn't getting any better. The hits kept coming; Fulton Brown continued to smile and focus on her second monograph on the Virgin Mary. She appeared to be having fun, despite the appalling things said about her. But, privately, friends were worrying about the toll it was taking, and on the damage it might be doing to her career.

One of the principal architects of Fulton Brown's *annus horribilis* was a then-unknown, untenured junior professor at Vassar College named Dorothy Kim. Kim had been goading Fulton Brown on social media for a year and a half, in an apparent attempt to get a rise out of the Chicago professor. Fulton Brown's riposte, when it finally arrived in September 2017, politely but firmly refused to concede any ground, directing those anxious about medieval history being used to shore up white supremacy to "learn some fucking history." Her post was decidedly light-hearted, as was its title: "How To Signal You Are Not A White Supremacist."

The language was even-tempered, too, given eighteen months of provocation and name-calling. "I'd better say something!" she wrote. "Here goes: 'I am not now, nor have I ever been a white supremacist.' You don't look convinced. What if I swear on a Bible? Heretics won't swear, they are famous for it. Except maybe I am a witch, and witches make false oaths all the time. And I am pretty sure that if you threw me in a swimming pool, I would float. Years of being on the high school swim team—it is a hard habit to break."

Her tone was indulgent, perhaps mildly amused, schoolteacher, rather than vicious racist instigator, but the mere act of publishing these words was seen by others in the field as courageous. Few academics, presented with a rapidly expanding cabal of furious on-

line critics and wild, unsubstantiated allegations fly-
ing around of "white supremacy" and racism, would
refuse to submit to the mob, instead thumbing their
nose at their angry critics. But that's what Fulton
Brown did.

All hell broke loose. Rather than respond to Fulton Brown's blog post, Kim deployed a time-honored
strategy for Leftist culture warriors caught with their
pants down: she claimed to be on the receiving end
of waves of harassment and racist abuse, which, she
alleged, was further inflamed when a website this author operated at the time covered the erupting row
as part of its campus controversy beat. Kim whipped
up a social media tornado, alleging that the tenured
Fulton Brown was responsible for organizing a tar-
geted campaign of harassment against a junior academic. What was amazing was that the hideous messages Fulton Brown started to receive came not from
anonymous accounts, but from the verified accounts
of other academics.

Fulton Brown was also accused of doxing, despite
only repeating materials Kim had personally published herself. What Fulton Brown had done was
quote Kim's own words back at her and rebut them,
illustrating her rebuttal with a readily publicly avail-
able official portrait of Kim—pertinent, because Kim
had written that her physical appearance suggested to

people that she wasn't a racist. But for some reason the story grew legs, and journalists started sniffing around, ears cocked for any headline into which they could crowbar a reference to white supremacy. The optics, as they say, weren't great.

II

BURN THE WITCH

In response to the startling claim that Dorothy Kim had suffered an avalanche of racially charged abuse and harassment, Fulton Brown did what historians do: she asked for evidence. And that's when Kim's story began to fall apart. First, Kim had claimed that the threats and harassment had come in via social media. When none could be found, the story changed: the threats had been sent in via email, and there had been prank calls.

Each time questions were raised about the new version of events, the explanation changed yet again: later, when Kim was asked to provide examples of the emails, or screenshots of them, she said she hadn't received them personally, but they had gone to her department marked for her attention. No one in the field had the courage to point out what was becoming obvious: it was probably all a lie.

It might seem churlish of Fulton Brown to insist on seeing evidence that a fellow female academic really did receive the harassment she claimed. In an ideal world, we would like to have faith enough in our fellow human beings to take such statements at face value. But the more she dug into the hysteria, and the inconsistencies in Kim's claims, the more questions she was left with about the Vassar professor's sincerity and credibility.

Seemingly in retaliation for being asked to provide evidence and being caught out, Kim began to claim ever wilder charges of harassment against Fulton Brown, and it became impossible to visit #medievaltwitter and not be sucked into the gruesome psychodrama. "The most recent incident I heard of concerned a conference session at which Dorothy claimed that Rachel had made some sort of hostile move against her and that she claimed she was worried about her physical safety," explains Jane Chance, a leading Tolkien scholar and the current Andrew W. Mellon Distinguished Professor Emerita at Rice University.

"She wanted Rachel barred from the session. But there were plenty of people at that session, and nothing happened. No one attacked Dorothy Kim. Kim seems afraid that trolls are going to come in and hurt her or kill her family or something. It's some kind of over-reaction to something she fears, and she sees this as directly related to her ethnicity. But Rachel has nothing to do with this, at conferences or otherwise."

Dorothy Kim was guilty of all the things she falsely accused Fulton Brown of doing to her: hurling abuse and name-calling, but also encouraging more of the same on social media via a tight-knit band of over-whelmingly male supplicants and quockerwodgers, who credulously accepted, or at least said they accepted, her allegations as fact. Buoyed by these pliant male attendants from minor New York schools, Kim overplayed her hand.

She began to claim, ludicrously, that having her own words quoted back at her alongside her photo-graph placed her in "physical danger," an escalation from the previous claim of doxing. And she started to slander Fulton Brown, through her intimates on social media, and herself, directly, from conference stages. As recently as July 2018, Kim was branding Fulton Brown a "fascist" on stage in front of an inter-national audience of her peers, who were asked not to record or report on the session. Obviously, it being a crowd of academics, someone did.

In the midst of this public conflagration, in which Fulton Brown was being openly slandered as a fascist and a racist, a public letter signed by 1,500 of Fulton Brown's colleagues scolded her for, in effect, being insufficiently woke on matters of social justice, and implied that she was a white supremacist. As an example of public shaming it was breathtaking in its scope and cruelty—and designed to terrify anyone inclined to support Fulton Brown.

The letter claimed that the professor had intervened "with ignorance into an already developed and nuanced scholarly conversation" and that "her ignorance of basic theoretical principles of race theory renders her an ill-informed and substandard interlocutor in the rigorous scholarly discussion of this important subject." In other words, Fulton Brown didn't use the right words, and didn't take the right positions on the issues, so she wasn't qualified to speak on the subject at all. If she'd been Hildegard of Bingen, claiming to be inspired by the Voice of the Living Light, she would have gotten a fairer hearing. But Fulton Brown is a white, Republican-voting Catholic convert from the Midwest, and she doesn't mind who knows about it.

Fulton Brown is also a substantial, serious and well-regarded academic. She commands intense respect and admiration from her peers for her work. Thomas Madden, Director of Saint Louis's Center for Medieval and Renaissance Studies and one of the most important medievalists in America, according to *Medieval Review*, described her scholarship to this author as "some of the most exciting and innovative work

produced in medieval studies today." Madden was ef-
fusive about her accomplishments. "I first contacted
Rachel in 2006 after reading a scholarly article that
she wrote in one of the most prestigious journals in
the field. The article was so perceptive, so empathetic,
and so groundbreaking that I had to look her up and
send her an email. I never do that!

"By then, I had already read her first monograph,
From Judgment to Passion, which I also found to be
an amazing achievement for an early career historian." The Medieval Academy of America awarded
that book the John Nicholas Brown prize, a highly
coveted honor. "Rachel's subsequent scholarship has
maintained that high bar," says Madden. "Her second monograph, *Mary and the Art of Prayer*, is a real
achievement. I have nothing but the highest regard
for Rachel's work."

Fulton Brown's first book won other awards, too,
including an award for the best book in intellectual
history published in 2002. And she has received
many honors and fellowships, not just for her scholarship, but also for her teaching, including a Guggen-
heim fellowship, two fellowships from the American
Council of Learned Societies, and two from the Andrew W. Mellon Foundation. But none of this made
a difference to the mob. Fulton Brown, an accomplished historian at the height of her intellectual and

academic powers, had done nothing wrong—and it seemed increasingly like Kim was a fantasist and a hypocrite—yet, for several weeks, it looked as though Fulton Brown's position in the history department at the University of Chicago, one of the country's most prestigious citadels of learning, might be at risk.

Dorothy Kim has published no books, though she regularly announces new forthcoming titles. Her publication history is essentially non-existent. Kim's sole claim to scholarly achievement appears to rest on a $200,000 National Endowment for the Humanities grant in 2012 to study medieval language, which she described, in 2014, as a work in progress. The grant period ran out in 2017, but in the seven years since she received the money, Kim is yet to demonstrate any progress.

It is sometimes mentioned by others, but never with a link to any evidence of work done. Its website is now defunct. No scholar I spoke with was aware of any work being published or prepared for publication to fulfill the promise of this large, taxpayer-funded grant. One of the few examples online of any substantial work being done is one 2010 undergraduate project supervised by Kim, documented on Vassar's website.

There are no consequences for failing to deliver projects paid for by the American public, though past performance is generally taken into account when awarding future money. But seemingly abandoned work like this is one of the reasons why the United States Congress regularly debates defunding the NEH. The misuse of taxpayer money alleged by some academics is especially galling, they say, in light of the fact that the *Internet Medieval Sourcebook*, still one of the most important resources online for medievalists since its first appearance in 1996, was famously self-funded as a labor of love by gay historian Paul Halsall.

Exactly why Dorothy Kim would launch an assault on a senior, respected female scholar in her own field remains a mystery to fellow medievalists, although some speculate it could be part of a larger war on traditional forms of research. Jane Chance lamented by phone from a hotel room in Atlanta, "I was so sad to see all this happen. I used to be friends with Dorothy. We both used to enjoy watching *Project Runway*. She always had something to say about the girls on the show.

"Rachel is held in very high esteem by the profession. She is the winner of a singularly meritorious award. Dorothy hasn't published anything substantial, and she is taking up all her time with scandals. You need calm and quiet to write, which she isn't giving herself," adds Chance, who says she takes no pleasure in the spectacle of Kim's self-immolation. "She has no idea how she has killed her career. Every time she disagrees with a woman now, people are going to wonder where it's coming from. They are going to see what she is really made of."

Fulton Brown has been subjected to vast quantities of the sort of abuse that Kim herself claimed to receive—even, astonishingly, spiteful comments on her physical appearance from fellow female academics. Some of the other women in Medieval Studies are aghast. "They called her ugly! Who does that?" exclaimed Jane Chance to me over the telephone. For briefly defending Fulton Brown, Chance was unfriended by one of the major characters in the story, Eileen Joy, who advertised the fact in a long post associating her and Fulton Brown with "ethnocentrism," and made the subject of dozens of colossal comment threads and arguments. It was a warning to others: stay away from the black sheep.

Unlike her critics, Fulton Brown conceals the names of fellow academics in many of her blog posts about the controversy. But internet records shared with this author show that Katharine Jager, an associate professor of English at the University of Houston-Downtown, called Fulton Brown "ugly" and that her face "morphed into horror." Jager says she "almost recoiled" at the sight of Fulton Brown—

but was quick to make clear that she didn't mean "to body shame in any way."

And Diane Berg, a graduate student at Tufts University, accused Fulton Brown of looking "snide" and of having an "imaginary boyfriend." These statements were posted publicly on Facebook, by women who have elsewhere identified themselves as feminists. Neither Jager nor Berg responded to a request for comment.

Eventually, the University of Chicago made it clear that they were not going to fire Fulton Brown. But her nightmare was really just beginning. Left-leaning critics say that abuse and harassment online have a chilling effect on the free speech of minorities, especially women. But none of Fulton Brown's critics have expressed the slightest concern or remorse about the legion of anonymous internet trolls who know a suspicious amount about the ins and outs of medieval studies—indeed, they seemed positively delighted that Fulton Brown was getting what she deserved.

Even when the facts became clear, and serious questions hung in the air about Kim's claims, no one would come to Rachel Fulton Brown's defense. To this day, the University of Chicago remains silent on the matter, and her department has done nothing besides issue a boilerplate statement distancing themselves from Fulton Brown's personal opinions. The

Medieval Academy of America, an academic body to which most medievalists belong, didn't punish Kim: instead, they rewarded her.

Kim was given free membership. Her fees were waived for life as "compensation" for her harassment ordeal, despite the fact that she has provided no evidence to substantiate the allegations she made against Fulton Brown—allegations which, in all likelihood, were fabrications. To many in the medievalist world, including half a dozen professors I have spoken with over the past few months, it appears as though the Academy has rewarded Kim for wantonly embarking on a mission to destroy a tenured professor's reputation with an ever-changing cornucopia of untruths.

"Dorothy Kim is a true believer on a crusade," Richard Landes, a renowned professor of history, wrote in response to questions about the controversy. "On the one hand, she's like the millennialists of the English Civil War, for whom any sign of hierarchy is a sign of Anti-Christ. Hence the anger against Fulton Brown speaking from a position of authority. At the same time, her language is authoritarian and categorical. Any disagreement is seen as proof of racism to be banished.

"Kim shares this with other intersectionalists, who think in Manichaean ways about the big issues, turning them into zero-sum battlegrounds in a war for their notion of justice. It is a fundamentally anti-academic approach ... a millennial authoritarian movement to weaponize knowledge, to advance passionately-held but often loopy notions about social justice."

Medieval Studies is an outlier in the academy. Although the foundational texts of medieval history are also the foundational texts of the academy itself, it has always been on the margins as a discipline. Since the founding of the Medieval Academy in America in 1925, it has been an interdisciplinary endeavor including language, literature, history and philosophy. Medieval scholars tend to reside in their parent disciplines: a medievalist based in a literature department will work on quite different projects, and use quite different language, to one reared in a history department.

As you might imagine, the scholars causing trouble teach English; their targets tend to be historians. Medievalist researchers from English departments are more interested in literary criticism and tend to be in conversation with English professors working on other periods, preoccupied with postmodernism and post-structuralism; historians have to learn how to talk to other historians. Though literature-based medievalists do have language skills—most understand Old English, for example—the historians usually pos-

sess the more powerful and wide-ranging scholarly
toolkits and intellects. Rachel Fulton Brown belongs
to the latter group.

Based on interviews I conducted over the course of
several months, the consensus in the Medieval Studies field is that literature departments lost the war
against identity politics and social justice decades ago,
so ambitious young academics from that world are
now looking elsewhere for new disciplines they can
conquer, with panels on the intractable problem of
whiteness and rarefied feminist readings of obscure
manuscripts. Professional cosmognosis propels these
entirely parasitic organisms into new growth vectors.
They arrive in a new discipline, claiming to speak for
the "marginalized" and "under-represented," publishing forceful denunciations of the usual boogeymen of
sexism, homophobia and white supremacy.

They make what at first appear to be fairly rea-
sonable requests for representation, but which later
metastasize into disproportionate amounts of airtime
dedicated to trivial or imaginary problems, and, of
course, to congratulating one another and hurling
specious, unchallenged and professionally devastating
allegations at unsuspecting colleagues. This is how
academic disciplines die. Richard Landes notes: "A
colleague of mine who started out in Race Studies,
and left the field, told me that whenever the conver-

sation turned to race, the collective IQ dropped ten points. The same thing is happening here."

Sharp-elbowed young professors know that a pre-occupation with social justice is both fashionable and advantageous. It can also excuse you from the pesky business of serious scholarly work. For academics lucky enough to belong to a "marginalized group," or who profess loudly enough to care about "the vulnerable", shrieking warnings about the appropriation of medieval studies by a vast, unseen white supremacist conspiracy out there in Trumpland is a more friction-free path to stage time and press attention than, say, burying one's head in Biblical exegesis. There are people incensed by this injustice, but, to their shame, not one of them has been brave enough to admit it publicly, except Rachel Fulton Brown.

Elitist educators are desperately anxious about their status and professional standing, and this informs their targets and tactics. Because academics are obsessed with prestige and respectability, any opportunity to present Rachel Fulton Brown as lacking in professorial gravitas in the months that have passed since her blog post about Dorothy Kim has been seized upon by a mob that includes graduate students and professors.

Dorothy Kim did not secure tenure at Vassar and has moved on now that her grant money has run out.

She has since been appointed at Brandeis University, which has a reputation for indulging identity politics and social justice demands to a degree considered extreme even by university standards, and her reckless language and risk-taking continue to worsen.

Social justice activists have a habit of not practicing what they preach. Fulton Brown's critics, for instance, have been repeatedly and ostentatiously guilty of the sins of which they accuse her, and in pathetically trivial ways. Medievalist Twitter erupted when Fulton Brown wrote the word "fucking." The offending phrase eventually even caught the eye of Mark Zuckerberg's sister Donna, who has founded her own online Classics magazine, *Eidolon*. (Yet another attempt by Classics to muscle in on Western civilization at the expense of the Middle Ages.) Zuckerberg took a class on Tolkien under Fulton Brown, but now describes that fact as "embarrassing."

Yet social justice ringleader, journal publisher and "para-academic rogue drone-strike machine"—her words—Eileen Joy, described to this author by many as a powerful person in the field, swears like an old fishwife on Facebook, branding strangers "wankmaggots." A July 12, 2018 post of Joy's describes her ideological opponents as "fuckheads," and concludes: "Just stop, you vile pieces of bodily matter that somehow missed the boat labelled 'human beings' when it

docked at your mothers' vaginas. Yeah.I.Said.That."
When I reached out to Joy for comment, she deac-
tivated her Facebook, for reasons that will become
obvious.

Somehow, Fulton Brown's exasperated entreaty to
"Learn some fucking history"—her point being that
learning the facts about the Middle Ages destroys any
white supremacist narratives—was taken as unprofes-
sional. Zuckerberg, who is proud enough of her PhD
to add "Dr." to her name on Twitter, did not respond
to a request for comment.

I have been getting to know the Professor over the
past three years, and we are now friends. She has
blogged dozens of times about me, my campus vis-
its, and my approach to defending free speech and
fundamental American freedoms on her website. She
makes no secret of her admiration and fondness for
me; I, likewise, cannot deny my admiration for her
determination in the face of overwhelming pressure
to swim with the tide, and her refusal to simply stay
silent as so many of her colleagues in the academy
have done. Much of the opprobrium heaped on her
has centered on our perceived friendship, operating
on the principle of guilt by association.

Fulton Brown's refreshing lack of snobbery and
her refusal to get angry infuriate her critics, few of
whom agreed to comment on the record for this

story, responding indirectly instead on Twitter, if they responded at all, invoking the imaginary terror of "harassment," "reprisals," "death threats" and "violence" and recycling bogus allegations of anti-Semitism against the author. The blizzards of invective and constant backbiting from the Left contrast beautifully with Fulton Brown's lifelong dedication to confelicity.

As I told the website *Campus Reform*, which reported on these allegations before this story was originally published, "You would expect academics, of all people, to take a breath before diving into the hysteria that has gripped society in the era of Trump. But, if anything, they are even more subject to moral panic and groupthink than reporters.... I am a Jew and an unreconstructed Zionist. I am married to a black man from Jersey. There aren't words for how deranged these allegations are." These are standard perils for anyone who contradicts the prevailing orthodoxy.

When we reached out to him for comment, abortion advocate, CNN guest blogger and former medieval professor David Perry seemed to confuse requests for comment with "calls for violence." Matthew Gabriele, a Virginia Tech professor best known for calling the NRA a "terrorist organization" but who is also a member of the Council of the Medieval

Academy of America, inexplicably wondered aloud whether he was being singled out for being Jewish.

After calling his ideological opponents, and especially Rachel Fulton Brown, supportive of and complicit with "white nationalists" and "anti-Semites," Gabriele has retweeted exhortations to "punch Nazis." More than one observer connected the dots: "How is this not a case of a white man calling for direct violence against a woman?" asked medievalist Paul Halsall.

Gabriele has executed a tight-rope act, acting civilly in professional environments while bomb-throwing online, as this third-party recording of a recent conference exchange between him and Fulton Brown at Emory University in Atlanta, Georgia shows. Alas, by his own logic, appearing to speak in a civilized manner to Fulton Brown without denouncing her as a Nazi has made him complicit. Of what, the jury is out. Rumor has it Gabriele has acquired the nickname 'Archangel' in medieval circles after leaping to the defense of so many needy damsels.

"Matt is brave on the internet," a tenured professor of history with several published books told me, "But a pretty sorry spectacle in real life. If you ask me, David Perry and Matt Gabriele are ticked off that they're not the only well-known medievalists on the internet. Of course, there are bigger fish around than them, but often those are men. And they haven't got the balls to go after a Holt or a Madden. They are perfectly happy to hound a woman they think they can intimidate, though."

People who spend their time online, attempting to destroy the reputations of those with whom they disagree politically, respond hysterically when someone dares to point it out. Overreactions to neutrally-worded requests for comment are a common feature of the American progressive Left, and their reaction to having their own words presented back to them can be instructive. The mere process of fact-checking this story was enough to produce the effect. And many of the characters approached for comment in this story began furiously back-pedaling their prior statements when news began to spread of its impending publication. This was not lost on hypocrisy-watcher Dan Franke, who is a history professor.

Many of the people named in this story were engaged in frantic, panicky deletions of, or revisions to, their most outrageous past statements as they became aware of its impending publication. I of course retain copies of all the statements to which I refer in this piece, and many more besides, edited out for reasons of space, and I am happy to provide copies to interested parties. As of July 29, 2018, Zuckerberg and Gabriele scoff at the idea that just because you're a medievalist, someone might think you're a white supremacist. That's a bad faith argument, they now claim.

Except that's exactly what Dorothy Kim said in the post that kicked off all the drama. She wrote: "You really have no excuse to address whether your medieval studies is a white supremacist medieval studies or not. You also do not have a choice in whether you are part of this debate because the debate is already prevalent and public. Our students are watching and will make judgements and calls on what side you are really on. I suggest overt signaling of how you are not a white supremacist and how your medieval studies is one that does not uphold white supremacy. Neutrality is not optional." It was a confessional exercise, and, until I first published this essay in July 2018, Zuckerberg and Gabriele, especially, shared Kim's position.

Other characters, such as medievalist professor and philodoxical blog baron Jeffrey J. Cohen, rushed to publish uncharacteristic entreaties to collegiality and politeness on their websites and social media. "Cohen, as much as anyone else in the field, is responsible for the current atmosphere of acrimony," I was told by a junior academic who agreed to speak more bluntly if we withheld his name. "And now he's calling for unity? I may never stop laughing." There is no more reliable emetic than 500 words of frantic back-pedaling from a Leftist activist who never anticipated journalistic scrutiny: by that measure, Cohen's blog is industrial-strength Ipecac.

Tellingly, many of the people we reached out to declined to comment unless we revealed which publication their words would appear in: not only were they worried about the professional impact of their own words appearing in a critical context in a publication read by their peers, but they were also, as one of them later confessed privately, planning to petition the editor to spike the piece.

The author did not reveal that this story was originally slated to appear in one of the country's most prestigious higher education publications. Who can say whether the furious briefing campaign from left-wing medievalists achieved its objective—but two days before publication, I was abruptly informed that the story would not run as intended, with no further explanation offered.

When news of this story spread to the press, the *Daily Beast*, which has a track record of running cover for far-left activists whose wrongdoing has been exposed, rushed out a feature alleging that the "alt-right"—a movement it had previously declared dead and buried—was "taking over Renaissance fairs." Rachel Fulton Brown has made no secret of her enthusiasm for Renaissance fairs and had attended one a week before the *Daily Beast* story was published. We are expected to believe that this is a coincidence.

The *Daily Beast* story itself is bizarre: you can count the number of unsavory characters at these events on one hand, and the examples the report offers are of medieval imagery, not racism. It mistakenly awards Dorothy Kim an associate professorship and its author seems to know nothing about history. There are a dozen examples of boneheadedness: the *Sonnenrad* is not a Nazi symbol; using Tolkien to bolster anti-Semitism is preposterous; the piece names just three people, in its long litany of racist horrors, who have ever been seen luxuriating in medieval iconography.

And the story claims that medievalists have not condemned white supremacy, which is simply an outright lie. The author cannot possibly believe it. Even Fulton Brown, who has resisted demands to pander to the confessional, or denounce her beliefs and her friends, has been unequivocal, in print, about her loathing of racists. Worst of all, perhaps, in the *Beast* report: the use of Walter Scott's *Ivanhoe* to promote white supremacy is left entirely unchallenged, despite the fact that the heroine of that story is Rebecca of York, a Jewess who saves Ivanhoe's life. Scott's whole point was to draw attention to the poor treatment of Jews by nineteenth-century England. This is precisely the kind of historical ignorance that Fulton Brown's "learn some fucking history" principle could have prevented. The story has been widely mocked on Twitter.

But the most absurd dimension of it all is that nothing associates the Middle Ages with white supremacy more than journalists and academics shrieking about it. By furiously denouncing white supremacy and its alleged fondness for the Middle Ages, reporters and professors have done far more to associate the two in the public's imagination than a hundred racist rallies in Charlottesville. And they know it, too. "The goal of social justice in Medieval Studies seems to be to have every professor of the subject impress upon vulnerable, impressionable and ignorant students the link between their subject and racism. Attempts to aggressively dissociate the two has the opposite effect. And that's the whole point," confided a distinguished professor.

The bad-faith, disingenuous hypocrisy of the Leftist tendency is why it is so immensely enjoyable to watch Fulton Brown respond good-naturedly to her ever-more-unhinged critics who believe, or say they believe, that a mild-mannered medieval historian's blog threatens their "physical safety." Those same critics haven't been afraid to publicly ridicule Fulton Brown, of course, and in some cases they have gone to extraordinary lengths to attempt to damage her professional reputation—and then denied it all and deleted their tweets when it looked as though their own words might be repeated back to them. "If the boot were on the other foot," said one journalist who covers university controversies for a national publication but who declined to be named, "They would be screaming blue murder. The hypocrisy is intolerable."

Dorothy Kim did not respond to an email requesting comment for this story. Two calls and an email to the Chair of English at Vassar College, asking why she was not offered tenure, and whether any prank calls, threats or harassing messages were received by her department, were not returned until just before publication, at which point Vassar's vice president of communications responded simply: "Vassar College does not comment on personnel matters." Poughkeepsie Police Department found no record of any harassment or death threat complaints made by Kim during the time she was employed by Vassar.

Since Fulton Brown and Kim met in the lists, panic has taken hold of the entire field of Medieval Studies. Fulton Brown has been asked not to attend conference sessions; conventions and congresses have been browbeaten into tearing up schedules to include more panels on diversity, inclusion, white supremacy and other social justice preoccupations; and senior figures in the discipline have taken vows of silence, terrified to say the wrong thing and risk destroying their reputations and legacies.

Dorothy Kim and her supporters ultimately failed to get Fulton Brown fired from the University of Chicago. Now their attention has turned to seeking out new victims. Grendel-like, the social justice pack is on the move, hungry for blood to avenge their wounded pride.

III

HOLY GRAIL

You might think Medieval Studies an odd place for a widespread social justice incursion. Perhaps the activists are just working their way down the list of university departments: they've conquered just about everywhere else, after all. As it happens, the invasion only really kicked off in 2010, much later than elsewhere in the humanities. Back then, prominent social justice blogger and academic Jeffrey J. Cohen could only muster 170 signatures for a letter demanding that the Medieval Academy of America move its conference from Arizona in protest at the state governor's immigration policies. At the time, the MAA held firm. Obviously, things have since changed.

Medieval Studies would be a glistering jewel in the social justice diadem, because study of the Middle Ages is fundamental to understanding how the Christian West emerged, and how dramatically its character differs from other cultures. Read prop-

erly, medieval history is about the divine comedy
of Christianity—and about the rise of its great eastern antagonist, Islam. Europe's self-criticism is what
medieval studies is largely about, so it stands at the
heart of current debates about Europe and western
civilization, including the current moral panic about
white supremacy.

The study of the Middle Ages is unavoidably
bound with nationalism as a discipline, since many
of the sources upon which it depends were first published in the nineteenth century, as part of great
national projects like the Rolls Series and the *Mon-
umenta Germaniae Historica*. Study of the period
demonstrates how central art and especially religion—
specifically Christianity—have been to the success
of the West. The Middle Ages stand as a foil to
modernity and a rebuttal to the spiritual coldness
of contemporary atheism and the creatively unsatis-
fying, logic-obsessed Anglo-American philosophical
tradition. *Pace* Gibbon, throughout the nineteenth
century, the Middle Ages were invoked to imagine
what Europe was really about, and who Europeans
were. You can see why the progressive Left wants to
tear it down.

Perhaps the reason it has taken this long for social
justice to spread here is something to do with the
enormously high technical skill required to operate in

the field. Medievalists have to be masters of hundreds of scholarly abilities, and most of them are proficient in half a dozen languages or more. Medieval Studies is aware of itself as a critical route to understanding the world, especially since 9/11. In the years since the attack on the Twin Towers, the relationships between Jews, Muslims and Christians has become ever more prominent in the public imagination. So, medievalists consider their discipline especially important today, and they are probably right to.

Given the centrality of Christianity in the Middle Ages and the current white supremacist witch-hunts in academia and the media, it's a wonder Leftists didn't come for medievalism sooner. In a way, this is the battle for which they have been sharpening their knives for decades. But they may find scholars in the field resistant. "Our professional survival does not depend on converting to a particular theory or methodology, especially at the cost of historical accuracy. To surrender accuracy and nuance, however good the cause may be, is to surrender the greatest tool our profession has to combat extremism," says Dan Franke. Not good news for critical theorists.

Eileen Joy has complained that people use medieval history as a "haven" to study white Christianity, as though there were something intrinsically objectionable about that, and ignoring the fact that Christianity was the culture of a largely fair-skinned Europe. According to Joy, the field is a "safe space to be elitist, a safe space to be white, a safe space to be Christian, Eurocentric, misogynist." But complaining about too much Christianity in Medieval Studies is analogous to objecting to too many numbers in math.

As Daniel Franke, an assistant professor of History watching the debate closely, has written for *Perspectives on History*, "However much we emphasize its breathtaking diversity and global connections, the historical fact remains that from around 1000 CE western European Christian society developed in ways connected to, but distinct from, other parts of the world. Simply establishing the widespread presence of non-'white' Europeans in medieval Europe is, as Fulton Brown argues, a powerful counter to white supremacist narratives of a racially 'pure' homeland." Franke had elsewhere referred to the social justice contingent in his discipline as the "Red Guard," after they invaded and ruined a well-known Facebook group. They didn't appreciate the joke.

Since 9/11, when the political Left redoubled its efforts to shore up Islam's reputation, medieval historians such as Jay Rubenstein have been representing the Crusades as a manifestation of white imperialism, expressing concern that Crusades scholarship and the depiction of the Crusades in culture has fed euro-centrism.   Opponents of this view, led by Florida State College professor and expert on the Crusades Andrew Holt, point out that they were defensive: Islam had been pushing against Christian Europe for centuries.

Left unstated by Holt—though not by Fulton Brown—is a more obvious, commonsensical objection: what's wrong, exactly, with euro-centrism? And aren't we glad the Christians won? Holt, not responding directly to this question, referred me to a Q&A on his website in which he describes Fulton Brown as a "leading medievalist" whose scholarship is "excellent" and "extensive," and another interview with Jane Chance.

There is an obvious moral dimension to medieval history denied by the culturally relativist Left: the Christians were the good guys. The academic Left typically regards sentiments like this as expressions of racism or calls for white ethno-states, continuing their decades-long conflation of "Western," "Christian," "capitalist" and "democratic" with "white." Professors from across disciplines support each other's efforts to associate the best of the West with bigotry and hatred, with Medieval Studies professors providing evidence from history and Religious Studies professors providing scriptural verisimilitude.

But people who actually do want white ethno-
states tend not to express themselves in terms of medieval history, even if they use images of twelfth-century
knights on their Twitter profiles. They much prefer
the Third Reich to the thirteenth century: medieval
imagery is a distant third to Nazism and the Holo-
caust in their vernacular and iconographic toolkits,
as alt-right websites and social media postings clearly
show.

Reached in Israel, Richard Landes explained that
the fight against euro-centrism has been spreading
through academia for decades. "We started with a
sort of modesty, suggesting to one another, 'Let's not
be so triumphalist.' But now the West is considered
the incarnation of all that's terrible. Even pointing
out that the West has valuable traits has become a
sort of hate speech. As the son of David Landes, I
went into academia to answer the question: 'Why
the West?' But when I was ready to start having my
say in the 1980s, the question I wanted to answer
was already off the table. Today, my father would
be considered a heretic."

"The Medieval West was full of 'us-them' thinking,"
he continued. "Some of it could be incredibly vicious,
especially the religious stuff. But so could the wars
between clans, between town and gown, and between
monarchs, for whom war was a personal sport. There

is much to condemn in medieval behaviors, but race is probably the least helpful way to think about them. We shouldn't lose sight of the fact that it was only in the West that a culture of openness, egalitarianism and mutual tolerance developed as far as it has. Medieval history is being used by some as fodder for racist attitudes. But you don't deal with that by cleansing Medieval Studies of anything that might be so used— for instance, the exceptional power and effectiveness of western culture."

Leftist medievalists seem to think that the appearance of a few Maltese crosses at racist rallies is evidence that any time medieval imagery appears online, in popular culture or in the news, it must be a sinister manifestation of white racism, that academic medievalists are somehow responsible for this awful trend, that academic medievalists can somehow stop it—and have a responsibility to do so—and that there is a vast white supremacy epidemic engulfing the country, reflective of and perhaps a product of their own discipline's unbearable whiteness.

Each of these propositions is individually ridiculous, yet entire conferences are now staged about the supposed co-option of the Middle Ages by racists and what the academy can do about it. Dan Franke preferred not to comment on the record for this story, but he objects strongly to the left-leaning analysis, and has written, "One would be very hard-pressed to find professional medieval historians, of whatever political persuasion, who taught a 'white nationalist' curriculum."

The racially-charged alt-right has adopted Crusader knight iconography. This is undeniable. But so have thousands of people who are merely skeptical of Islam. I confess to being personally responsible for the renewed popularity of the phrase "Reclaim Constantinople" since I dedicated a college talk to the subject in December 2016. The talk was illustrated with a photo of a stars-and-stripes emblazoned MOAB hanging in the air over the Kaaba. And so have many people in America and throughout Europe in the newly energized populist Right-wing, a political uprising which is much less squeamish about celebrating the cultural and economic superiority of the West than other recent strands of conservatism.

Lots of people are drawn to medieval imagery, usually not for nefarious reasons. Seeing lots of Crusader iconography around and concluding there is a national outbreak of white supremacist militants isn't concerned scholarship: it's the fallacy of composition. Just because you've seen a handful of deluded racists with Chinese-made tiki torches and fiberglass broadswords, doesn't mean that every time you see any artistic, linguistic or historical reference to the

Middle Ages that the person responsible is a white nationalist—unless you are one of those absurd individuals who believes that every one of the 63 million people who voted Republican at the last election is a closet racist, in which case what you really need is a good apothecary.

IV
HUE AND CRY

A typical claim of the social justice tendency in Medieval Studies is that scholars should widen their focus out from Europe and into Eurasia and Africa. They say limiting your study of the Middle Ages to Europe is too "white-centric." But almost everyone teaching the Middle Ages has taught courses on pilgrims, preachers, and travelers to Asia like William of Rubruck and Marco Polo.

Left-wing medievalists like to exclaim, "The Middle Ages weren't only in Europe," a fatuous claim which appears to mean, "Don't forget that the rest of the world existed." There's no evidence anyone ever has forgotten—and besides, applying the term Middle Ages to contemporary China would be something like cultural imperialism, according to the progressive inquisitor's manual.

Scholars of the Middle Ages are acutely aware that Europe was a backwater—just as the people living in

Europe themselves were, which is why so much medieval history focuses on the experiences of Europeans in the Middle Ages stunned by the size and sophistication of Eastern cities. Constantinople was considered the center of civilization; Jerusalem was placed in the middle of every *mappa mundi*. Paradise was located in Asia. "It is farcical to suggest that people who study the Middle Ages don't know this," says Fulton Brown.

Insufficient attention is paid in medieval curricula to the "problem of whiteness" and its complicity in European slavery, the same critics claim. But the medieval slave trade stretched from Scandinavia to the furthest reaches of the Muslim world. Vikings began their raids not for food or precious metals, but to abduct people they could sell into servitude. Globally speaking, slavery isn't a "white thing"—it wasn't in the Middle Ages and it isn't now. There isn't a scholar in the field who doesn't know about slavery in the Middle Ages, or a student who leaves college not learning about it.

As is so often the case with progressive academics, critics of medieval history aren't telling anyone anything new—they're just aggressively insisting on a change in emphasis without giving persuasive reasons for their demands. Many in the field suspect, and told me as I was researching this story, that Leftist critiques of the field seem to have less to do with rebalancing a Euro-centric understanding of the past than they do with giving white Christian Europe—and, by implication, modern Christian America—a bad name, just as Leftist academics have been doing for decades in other academic disciplines.

It's true that there are relatively few people of color in Medieval Studies, if you don't count the Green Knight. It's less clear why that is: possibly, black academics just aren't as interested in European history as they are African. Or perhaps Medieval Studies is failing to recruit black academics because its most prominent professors are Left-wing cultural critics anxious to distance themselves from the one dimension of their discipline that might actually appeal to African-Americans: Christianity. And maybe Asian scholars are drawn to subjects outside the humanities entirely.

But the relative whiteness of Medieval Studies doesn't, in and of itself, prove any innate hostility to marginalized communities. Critics from within Medieval Studies claim they are made to feel unwelcome, or that they are driven out of the field. But it's far from obvious why that might be. Academia is a brutal environment, after all. "You're constantly being judged," says Fulton Brown, who sympathizes with colleagues who feel bruised by the peer review process. "But that's what academia feels like for everyone. And you're being assessed by people who don't tell you who they are. It's highly competitive and very stressful."

There's no more evidence for the claim that Medieval Studies is actively hostile to minorities than there is for the less generous view that mediocre performers are always on the look-out for excuses for their own failure. The progressive consensus on campus and in wider American culture provides dozens of ready-made victim scripts for stressed, worn-out people. There's no reason to suppose it's all down to racism and sexism when there are much simpler and more convincing explanations. Professors are only human, and those who find the realities of academia too much to bear can be tempted to find reasons for their failure or stress levels, just like anyone else in any other kind of job.

Dan Franke has tweeted, "The crying shame of it all is that Medieval Studies is already one of the most welcoming, inclusive fields of academia. We have long been open to experimentation and novel approaches." What Franke doesn't realize, perhaps, is that social justice warriors don't go where they are needed—they go where they are powerful. Hence the concentration of LGBT activists, gender warriors and race-baiters in places where people are more easily intimidated, and already likely to lean leftwards: university departments, Hollywood, the media and the charitable sector.

Academia in general is a rich and warmly inviting environment for women and minorities, because university departments aggressively solicit non-white and non-male applicants. Allegations that Medieval Studies is somehow hostile to women, or that it suppresses female voices, don't hold water: today the field is dominated by female academics. Claims that Medieval Studies professors are just as backstabbing and careerist as those in the rest of the academy, however, would appear to be true. For every Julian of Norwich, there is a Countess Mahaut of Artois.

Most of what the millennial medievalists have been doing has played out on social media, in view of progressive journalists who have egged them on. Some of it is exhausting to follow. But the pattern follows other invasions by activists into genteel disciplines: lots of angry posts about "microaggressions" and demands for special treatment, followed by Twitter accounts being locked, Facebook groups splintering or shutting down entirely, and bewildered and terrified academics simply retreating from social media entirely and handing the playing field to the insurgents.

Fulton Brown has been the primary target, though she is rarely referred to by name, and instead in other disobliging ways, which change constantly to make searching for discussion of her as difficult as possible. Some of the more repeatable have included "RFB,"

"Famous Medievalist," and "She Who Shall Not Be Named." But some of the worst stories come from graduate students, who are easily browbeaten into saying they accept terminology and priorities handed out to them by schoolmarmish busybodies.

There is always the implied threat of what will happen if the tenets of social justice are not obeyed. Frequently, apologies are extracted from bewildered—and innocent—peers, through the use of allegations including but not limited to sexism, racism, neo-Nazism, white supremacy and anti-Semitism.

Eileen Joy, in particular, has been repeatedly accused of publicly naming graduate students "in order to extract confessions" over imagined grievances. "She puts Bernard Gui to shame," said one academic I spoke to who insisted his name not be used. (This is slightly unfair—to Gui. Church inquisitors believed in giving accused heretics the chance to prove themselves innocent before they passed judgment, unlike many secular judges, and Eileen.) According to private messages seen by this author, Dorothy Kim has also been guilty of strong-arming graduate students and attempting to stymie their professional advancement for the crime of disagreeing with her on the internet.

Unlike Kim, who seems as much a victim of identity politics as anyone, Eileen Joy has a formidable mind, capable of strategy, subtlety and compassion.

In the course of writing this story, I had long, detailed email correspondence with Joy, who emerged as a sincere and complex figure, aware of the gulf between her academic persona and the character she plays on social media. Joy clearly hates authority, especially Christian and male authority, and sees herself as a champion of the downtrodden.

But she appears not to appreciate that her own behavior can be far more toxic and chilling than the white male patriarchy against which she rails. Joy wrote to me at length, clearly wanting to be understood. And it worked: I found her much more relatable by the end. She would not give me permission to reproduce her emails, in which she makes a powerful case for her brand of burn-it-all-down activism. Nor would she allow me to share her thoughts on free expression and the state of the academy in general or Medieval Studies in particular. Nor would she respond to any of the charges made against her by her peers.

Joy's reluctance to comment came down to what people would think if she gave comment on the record to a story by me. She claims she doesn't care what other people think about her, but that's not true. She cares very much about the opinions of the few dozen perpetually furious online activists, including Cohen, Gabriele and Perry, upon whom her power

depends. They are all men, and they are all observ-
ably much less intelligent than she is and much less
capable of nuanced debate. Each of them would be
furious at her for speaking to me on the record.

Staying in their good graces by refusing to comment was ultimately more important to her than an-
swering the very serious charges of bullying and professional misconduct laid at her door by her fellow
academics—but also, and more importantly, making
her case for better representation in the field and more
attention paid to minority concerns. That's a shame,
because the Eileen Joy the world doesn't see—the Joy
behind the furious Facebook posts and the intimidation of graduate students and the smearing of colleagues and denunciations of conference organizers—
is a person who would win converts to her cause by
the thousand.

…at least, that's what I thought during our pro-
tracted, long-form correspondence. As it turned out,
the very same day Joy was complimenting me on my
questions, perhaps in the hope of flattering me into
softening my critique, she was sending letters threatening to sue the University of Chicago for somehow
being "directly responsible" for this story repeating
her own words back to her, "facilitating … cyberharassment." In the topsy-turvy world of social jus-

tice, reporting is abuse, journalism is harassment and
political dissidence is a capital crime.

A copy of Joy's letter was leaked to me by two
sources. I reprinted it in full on *dangerous.com*. It is
well worth reading in its entirety. While we were in
correspondence, I was unaware of Joy's legal threats to
the University; we continued to email for several days.
Joy forbade me from reproducing the contents of our
emails. I will not violate the agreement I made with
her. But she did also specifically recommend that I
give my impression from the conversation in place of
quoting her, and I am happy to do so. Any direct
quotes in what follows come from the Chicago letter,
and not from our private correspondence.

In her letter to Fulton Brown's employer, the measured, sophisticated academic of our email exchanges
is gone, replaced by a hysterical identity politics huck-
ster familiar from Facebook. But Joy was able to code-
switch between the two personalities effortlessly from
one hour to the next. The same day she was privately
dismissing the reputation of gay medievalist Paul Halsall in starkly homophobic terms that referred explicitly to a chronic health condition he is known to suffer
from, she was concocting elaborate excuses for what
she implied was effectively a drag persona on social
media.

Within that same twenty-four hour period, Joy also was mawkishly describing herself to University of Chicago dons as the victim of "frighteningly misogynist … men from the dark corners of the alt-right internet." This is the same Eileen Joy who had previously referred to Fulton Brown as a "hag" in a now-deleted Facebook post.

Privately, between reminding me how famous and influential she was, and complimenting her own fearlessness and indefatigability, Joy gave me essay-writing tips and defended queer readings of the Middle Ages while plaintively explaining why she sounded different on the internet to real life—and, excruciatingly for both of us, comparing herself to me. Just one of several rambling self-justifications for her acid tongue on the web ran to 1,185 words, in which Joy appeared desperate for me to appreciate her as part performance artist and part Marvel superhero. I'm not convinced.

Yet, at the very same time, in her letter to Chicago, Joy raged that the mere act of fact-checking this story—just receiving emails from this reporter—had contributed to an atmosphere of "insanity" that was "deeply dehumanizing." But who had truly been guilty of dehumanizing others? The journalist asking for comment, or the feminist medieval historian who intimidated graduate students on the internet and referred to other women as hags? Duplicity is a strong word, and yet it doesn't quite seem to do justice to this sort of shameless dissembling.

While she wrote to me privately invoking a desire to write and practice her craft without interference, and alluding to her belief in a broad church of possible medieval study modes, we now know Joy was, at the exact same time, maliciously intimidating Rachel Fulton Brown's employer and suggesting she might try to bring criminal charges against Fulton Brown, in a letter she strongly hinted she intended to publish, perhaps as revenge for finally being held to account for her sins, but ultimately for no better reason than Fulton Brown doesn't share her politics and is too hung up on the God stuff.

Her claimed apanthropy is pure fiction: if Eileen Joy craved scholarly solitude, she wouldn't spend hours every day on the internet, mercilessly policing the language and behavior of other women. To Joy, "being left alone to do my own thing" seems to mean "getting everything I want, all the time, or else."

It was only after our email exchange had been going on for some time—the day before this story appeared, in fact—that I was sent, from two sources, the complete email Joy had sent to the University of Chicago threatening them with a lawsuit and claiming she held them "personally responsible" for the conflagrations she had herself ignited in the field with her spiteful language and addiction to lobbing grenades at other people. She had sent the email, which referred to me as a "so-called 'journalist,'" whose neutrally-worded requests for comment were supposedly "beyond intimidating," less than five hours after emailing me at length and promising to eventually provide a comment I might be able to use on the record. No such comment ever arrived.

Her letter to Chicago, titled "Potential Lawsuit: Rachel Fulton Brown," threatens legal action several times while alleging "among other things, libel, cyberharassment, and reckless endangerment." She directs the University to "get some kind of handle on Prof Brown," presumably meaning either restrictions on Fulton Brown's First Amendment rights or outright termination. She describes Fulton Brown, in language worthy of a handkerchief-wafting Victorian noblewoman, as "a menace and a fear in our lives," as though she were Jack the Ripper in his heyday.

"Please help me," Joy intones in her Chicago letter. "Return my, and others' lives, back to 'normal.'" The evidence she presents for her allegation that Fulton Brown has torn her life apart are that Fulton Brown screenshotted Joy's own words and presented them for discussion. The chutzpah on show in Joy rebranding her own favorite object of slander and scorn as some kind of harassment architect is jaw-dropping, and the absurd legal threats in this long and unintentionally hilarious note suggest the real function of this letter: to punish Fulton Brown, yet again, and perhaps to stymie the release of the story you are reading now. Those familiar with the phrase "cry-bully" will understand the sort of cognitive dissonance on display. Joy would be wise to remember the old adage: don't start what you can't finish.

Joy made space for the old chestnut about "primarily target[ing] women of color and also women who are queer," too, falling back on one of the most pervasive and irritating habits of identity politicking. Because Fulton Brown disagrees with you, it must be because you're gay. "It couldn't possibly be, could it, that Eileen Joy behaves like a narcissistic, hypocritical oaf and a bully and is regularly busted giving different groups of people totally different accounts of the facts? No. Must be because you sleep with women." Needless to say, the source of that bon mot requested his name be withheld.

No social justice missive would be complete without two essential rhetorical flourishes: a shovelful of self-pity, and a reminder that it's all Donald Trump's fault. Joy does not disappoint: "The election of Donald Trump," she says, gave license to "angry white men to get angrier and angrier." She adds: "I am technically in a somewhat precarious position. My entire career has been building to this moment and I have also been without institutional employment and security since August 2013. Prof. Brown's actions are a potential threat not only to my mental well-being, but because all of these comments are public and online, my reputation and my future plans are threatened."

V

HIGH HORSES

Every now and then, the warriors get a trophy—sometimes a big one. Allen J. Frantzen, a professor who retired after 35 years of teaching in 2014, was called to task in late 2015 for a blog post on his personal website in which he referred to "feminist fog." He described modern feminism as a "sour mix of victimization and privilege"—hardly a controversial assessment in wider society, but an incendiary one to make in academia. "Anytime you challenge any aspect of feminism," he told the *Chronicle of Higher Education*, "You're going to hear that you hate women. I think this is the standard response to anyone that wanders off the reservation. I don't think they are doing a really great job at responding to my ideas."

Frantzen is gay, one of a number of homosexual men breaking free from the progressive consensus in the past decade. Gay women, like Eileen Joy, for some reason always seem to be social justice warriors. And he had written extensively about homosexual prejudice in his scholarly work. But that didn't save him from the scolds: Eileen Joy wrote that Frantzen's post was a "car crash" and started to give lectures during which she also accused him of plagiarism.

Jeffrey Cohen said the whole affair was "traumatic." Petitions and statements were circulated. Students and professors began proudly advertising the fact that they would no longer reference his work. Frantzen's scholarly reputation, earned over decades, was destroyed thanks to a blog post—and for little more than making a few trenchant observations about the excesses of feminism and for, in his words, "trying to build men up."

In July 2017, an international medievalist conference in Leeds was overshadowed by scandal when a German scholar made a light-hearted joke about not being tan enough. He was a white man speaking on a panel about "otherness," and he entreated any audience members uncomfortable with that to "wait until after his summer holiday." It was the most benign humor imaginable. But the social justice warriors lost their minds. Eileen Joy tweeted, suggesting it was the product of racism.

It became clear that critical faculties were being suspended, to say nothing of senses of humor, when complaints were made about the fact that book exhibitors at the Leeds conference were displaying

Celtic crosses and Viking paraphernalia. Apparently, not even people in the field were allowed to embrace the symbols of their own area of research any more. It was just too dangerous.

After Charlottesville, the signal-to-noise ratio became intolerable. Everywhere you looked, medievalists were genuflecting. The use of medieval imagery by racists prompted an outpouring of exaggerated hand-wringing, soul-searching and disgust. But only for a day or two. After that, it was back to waging war and publishing confused op-eds which seem at once to defend history from ignorant appropriation of white supremacists at the same time as demanding that scholars working in the field be committed to doing something about racism.

"It was never made clear what that 'something' ought to be," said one junior academic who would not even give me his name. "But judging by the activities of the ringleaders, it probably involves calling people 'Nazi' on the internet a lot."

Professor Carol Symes reflects the beliefs of the activist contingent in Medieval Studies when she claims that there is no way to "responsibly" engage with the subject without discussing its "modern and postmodern entanglements" and deploying critical theory, i.e., gender and race studies. Plenty of medieval historians simply disagree. But what they object to even more is that the social justice crowd are denying others the right to practice their own discipline in their own way—and seeking to destroy anyone who dares to dissent.

"Academic freedom includes the moral and professional right to disagree over the history of the profession, the choice and use of theory, and the interpretation of the past," as Dan Franke puts it. But Symes and her ilk say there are no two sides to the debate. She said that the "white supremacist, nationalist strains in medieval historiography ... will continue to support [racist] appropriations unless they are honestly addressed."

Symes, an associate professor at University of Illinois at Urbana-Champaign who studies history through a sociological lens, dedicated hundreds of words to attacking Fulton Brown in a blog post for the American Historical Association titled, "Medievalism, White Supremacy, and the Historian's Craft," accusing Fulton Brown of "deriding, bullying, and persecuting a junior, untenured medievalist of color." Reached for comment, she disputed the characterization of Fulton' Brown's blog posts and social media activity "as either measured or light-hearted," adding: "It is precisely because Professor Fulton-Brown is a respected senior scholar, with a secure tenured post at an elite institution, that she has a professional responsibility to use her privileged position to nurture and support junior colleagues who do not enjoy such privileges."

Symes appears to believe that this professional obligation should extend even to those junior colleagues who machinate to destroy one's career. No such protestations about good treatment to juniors were forthcoming from Carol Symes, or anyone else, when Dorothy Kim and Eileen Joy were intimidating graduate students on Facebook. But Symes, while stopping short of admitting she was duped, has since expressed some regret for her part in the witch hunt and has privately apologized to Fulton Brown.

Asked whether Dorothy Kim's failure to produce any evidence of harassment or abuse and the statements from Vassar College and Poughkeepsie Police Department changed her opinion of Kim, she insisted that it did not, but she also expressed surprise that the open letter to Fulton Brown's department had attracted so many signatures.

In conjunction with online campaigns designed to shame and intimidate, conferences and panels at larger conventions addressing the "whiteness" of the field are proliferating. Critics are discouraged or even forcibly prevented from attending. At the 2018 International Congress on Medieval Studies, Dorothy Kim requested that Fulton Brown be banned from attending the panel she was co-hosting. There are also workshops, support groups and a growing body of literature.

Meanwhile, according to screenshots and documents saved by her allies, suggestions that Fulton Brown's speeches should be protested, boycotted and "glitter-bombed" have been enthusiastically spread on Facebook by the same circle of activist-researchers—including Jeffrey Cohen, who was recently appointed Dean of Humanities in the College of Liberal Arts and Sciences at Arizona State University—only to be denied and played off as "jokes" when it became clear there was no appetite for such disruption. Cohen's appointment at Arizona State is ironic, given his aforementioned letter-writing campaign against the 2011 meeting of the Medieval Academy of America in Tempe.

Most recently, Eileen Joy, whose activist group is called BABEL (Americans pronounce this "babble"), posted, on the 2018 International Congress on Medieval Studies' Facebook page, in giant white lettering with a hot pink background, "Fuck the Kalamazoo Congress Committee & you know exactly why. You are complete and total reprehensible assholes." The ICMS's crime? They had declined to accept a panel suggestion from her group about "white allies" in

Medieval Studies. The other panel they had proposed was accepted.

An ICMS spokeswoman told the press in the aftermath that workshop selections were based on criteria such as "the intellectual justifications offered for individual sessions" and "the balance of topics addressed." Ouch! BABEL, using a letter drafted by Julie Orlemanski, publicly shamed the International Congress on Medieval Studies. The letter got 600 signatures in a matter of days. "Petition" is something of a euphemism, of course, because alongside this comparatively placid letter, posts on social media got increasingly more threatening, demanding and horrible.

The unnecessarily combative atmosphere and occasional outright abusiveness brought to the debate by Eileen Joy and her BABEL group has disturbed many in the field. At a previous ICMS, Joy had delivered a talk titled, "Fuck This Shit: How Can You Not Say Something?," but this is on the milder end of her scale of self-expression. Jane Chance, a former friend of Joy's, has been working on gender in the Middle Ages for decades—and she once sued Rice University over gender discrimination. In other words, her feminist credentials are impeccable. Chance can't work out what has happened to her old chum.

"Eileen Joy used to be a friend of mine, and I still sit on a board with her. But I was accused by Eileen of being a terrible feminist. I know a lot of people who will side with Eileen, because she is a powerful person, and her work is so good, but she has started alienating people right and left, using profanity and resorting to the sort of things that do not pass for civilized behavior." That's a sentiment echoed by most of the scholars interviewed for this story.

"Eileen has been touted as an 'it' girl, so perhaps she is surprised at not getting everything she wants," Chance confides. "But there's limited space at conferences. Not everyone gets to do all the things they want. And she got one of the two spots she asked for, so I really don't get it. She is being irrational and unremitting, and I don't think that ultimately Michigan will tolerate it. She isn't going to win this way. Besides, I'm sure she considers Kalamazoo as too traditional and fundamentally uninteresting." Chance can be forgiven for that last point of confusion: it's Kalamazoo's prestige that attracts the social justice warriors. Because to know they can warp the priorities of Medieval Studies' most influential annual conference is to know they are on their way to fully conquering the field.

A week or so before we went to press with the first edition of this essay in July 2018, the International Congress on Medieval Studies announced it would be rethinking its selection process, in light of BABEL's demands which had been countersigned by 600 others working in the field. Joy responded saying she wouldn't be attending anyway, accusing the conference of being hostile to people of color and gays. In other words, having damaged the reputation of the conference, soured the atmosphere with self-congratulatory fulmination and then getting the changes she had insisted upon, Joy took the opportunity to heap further unfounded name-calling and threats on the conference and declare she would not attend.

Others followed suit with cancellations and further condemnations. The world of Medieval Studies will therefore be tragically robbed of BABEL's insights into how white people can be better "allies." In case you're wondering, it involves a lot of nodding along and shutting up but stops just short of requiring a cilice.

VI

HUNDRED YEARS'
WAR

The reputation of American higher education has taken a battering—probably justifiably—in recent decades, thanks in large part to the excesses and absurdities of its humanities departments. Stories about outlandish pronouncements from Gender Studies professors are gleefully catalogued by conservative journalists, as are panicky, fact-free conspiracy theories about white supremacy—despite the fact that there are probably, at most, a couple of thousand genuine white supremacists in the entire United States. Witch-hammerer Heinrich Kramer had a less active imagination than your average associate professor of English.

The glamor and admiration once associated with higher education is evaporating, now that universities are seen as hyper-partisan centers of political indoctrination and fortresses of elitist hypocrisy. Reports from Right-wing media focus on professors who are just as wacky in real life as they sound on the page, and there is a rising suspicion in the U.S. that college isn't worth the money, and that parents would serve their children better by investing in their future some other way. This sentiment is not exclusive to Trump supporters. Public opinion of universities has never been more hostile.

College professors are themselves entirely responsible for this miserable state of affairs. First, out of complacency, they handed over the reins of their institutions to ill-qualified administrators, who set about making work for themselves by erecting gigantic bureaucracies, often parallel and entirely irrelevant to the business of learning. Then, educators refused to defend their own academic freedom from the rising tide of political correctness, social justice, victimhood culture and millennial entitlement that has crippled so many American colleges. The faculty has no one to blame but itself for the humiliating series of headlines: the Weinsteins at Evergreen State; Michael Rectenwald at NYU; Amy Wax at Penn Law; Tony Esolen at Providence; Paul Griffiths at Duke Divinity and of course the parallel universe that is Hallowe'en at Yale.

Academics aren't paid much, and most of them don't seem to mind, having taken a vow of poverty to their colossally rich institutions. They remain high

PUGET SOUND

UNDERWRITERS, INC.

520 PIKE STREET
SUITE 2120
SEATTLE, WA 98101

CAROL H. GARLAND

CPCU

Direct: 206-708-2048
Tel: 206-708-2000
Fax: 206-708-2001
1-800-767-9582
carol_garland@psuinc.com

UNDERWRITING MANAGERS
SURPLUS LINE BROKERS
LLOYD'S CORRESPONDENTS

in social capital, at least on campus. Yet they have done little to hang on to, and much to sacrifice, the one thing they truly value: prestige. Professors could have put their foot down at any point in the last three decades, when it was becoming clear that newly empowered students, who saw themselves as paying customers first and bookworms second, and administrators, desperate to discover a worthwhile function to justify their huge salaries, together began to create an atmosphere on campus that was deeply hostile to imaginative free-wheeling. But they didn't, and many educators now fear it is too late to arrest the decline.

In the wider discussion on campus freedoms, Chicago has said a lot of the right things when asked. But given a chance to put its "no safe spaces, no trigger warnings" philosophy into action, the institution failed. Not only did it fail to stand up for the academic freedom of a faculty member who was being assailed by forces hostile to free expression, but Fulton Brown's history department even published a cloying diversity statement after the controversy effectively capitulating to the manic left's definitions of harassment and sounding indistinguishable from any other university in kowtowing to the PC police.

The reaction from academics to Rachel Fulton Brown was spectacularly nasty, not only because she violated the tenets of social justice and political correctness by lightly mocking their obsession with "dead straight white males." She also did something far worse. She became notable, and notability, which can lead to fame, is something every academic heaps scorn on while secretly craving. The only thing more popular in faculty lounges than cheap red wine is vicious sniping at members of the guild who command an audience outside the academy.

The strongest passion in the academy—perhaps the only one left—is envy. And the impression I got while researching this story is that these scholars envy Rachel Fulton Brown. By developing a large following and refusing to follow the politically correct consensus, Fulton Brown had made herself a target for gossip, envy and bitterness. And when she refused to be cowed into silence by intimidation and public shaming, that sealed her fate. She had become a latter-day Marguerite Porete—fair game for professional annihilation.

As we have seen already, academic resentment can manifest itself in comically trivial ways. Julie Hofmann, a professor at Shenandoah University who blogs at *Another Damned Medievalist*, mockingly welcomed Fulton Brown to the online medievalist community a full ten years after she had begun writing online, suggesting Fulton Brown hadn't been noticed before because she hadn't attended "advertised blogger meet-ups at all the major conferences." The implication was that Fulton Brown wasn't a "proper" blogger because she hadn't paid her dues at meet-ups and therefore wasn't part of the respectable inner circle of medieval bloggers. What it really means is that she hadn't spent enough time as lady-in-waiting at Blog Court. Hofmann's blog has received 54,000 pageviews since 2002. Fulton Brown's *Fencing Bear at Prayer* has received 2 million in the last 24 months alone.

The fact that so many academics have unwisely piled on in this terrifying attempt to condemn a respected scholar speaks to the moral panic taking hold on campuses about the specter of white supremacy. 1,500 professors signed a letter denouncing Fulton Brown on the basis of events which in all likelihood simply did not happen. The organizer of at least one other open letter about Fulton Brown, Julie Orleman-ski, did not respond to a request for comment and has made no effort to apologize or make amends. None of the professors we contacted whose name appear on the open letter responded to requests for comment except one.

VII

HOLY, HOLY, HOLY

The cost of giving in to this wave of activist scholarship could be enormous. Richard Landes told me: "The effort to purge the ranks of scholars who fail to denounce perceived racism is simply bullying. The intersectionalists are actually the specific heirs to a Western egalitarian tradition with no parallels. To turn on the culture that produced you and label it the origin of all evil is a sort of oedipal auto-cannibalism that literally cuts off inspiration at its source.

"This is particularly important today, precisely as the West is under attack from the ferocious 'us-them' culture. It's like going out into a snowstorm wearing a bathing suit or disarming yourself before battle. Those people who invoke crusader themes and vote for belligerent candidates represent a—not always sound—response to the terrible failure of their supposed elites to defend the very culture from which they so benefit. The tribal responses in the West are natural self-defensive reactions, not pretty from the

progressive virtue-signaling perspective, but at some
defensive level both healthy and important. Instead
of helping, or even leading the defense of western
civilization, progressive elites leave the commoners to
fend for themselves, encourage the invading enemy,
and then heap contempt on their own people for
'white racism.' "

Ironically, given its marginality in the modern
academy, Medieval Studies has given birth to some of
the most enduringly destructive currents in intellectual history. As Bruce Holsinger has shown, French
postmodernist theory was invented by people who
were trained as medievalists and who were excited
by the multiple layers of meaning in medieval texts.
Barthes, Derrida, Bourdieu and Lacan all had some
degree of familiarity with the Middle Ages.

This provides further insight into the determination of social justice warriors to conquer medieval
studies. "Postmodernism lives or dies on this mountain, and so does the Left," explains Fulton Brown.
"Progressive academics unraveling Medieval Studies
would be the academic equivalent of ISIS sacking the
cathedral of Notre Dame in Paris. If Islamic terrorists
blow up Chartres, they win."

"This is why the West is so weak right now," she
continues. "Because it cannot defend itself, its own
tradition, without the Middle Ages. Even those who

want to defend the West start with the Enlightenment, with reason and logic. But the Enlightenment
without its creative, religious or artistic past cannot
defend itself. Our artistic tradition is focused on
worship. Our artistic, musical and dramatic tradi-
tions are all groundless without an understanding that
they were created in order to worship God within
the Christian church, standing before the throne of
God and singing, 'Holy, Holy, Holy is the Lord God
Almighty.' "

All great western art gestures toward the moment
Fulton Brown is describing: the *Liebestod*, Rem-
brandt, Rodin, Botticelli, Van Gogh, Bach, Mahler,
Coleridge, Shakespeare and Baudelaire, all the way
down to the last few impressionistic lines of a Larkin
poem. The awful, sick-making sadness wrapped in
loss and longing, and the helpless disorientation and
paralysis known to the Germans as *Sehnsucht* is en-
coded in two simple words, "That vase," at the end of
Larkin's poem "Home is so Sad." It is a moment the
whole world falls away and a brief gateway to Heaven
opens, if you know how to use it.

What sets the western tradition apart is precisely
that longing for the ineffable, the gasp, the lurch
toward the Almighty—a reach for the divine in the
hope of momentary contact. This brief, transcendent,
uplifting split second is what lovers of western art

and music chase, and it is present throughout both high- and lowbrow culture. A better-known example from Larkin, at the conclusion of "The Whitsun Weddings," captures the impossibly complex feeling at the center of the western tradition in four agonizingly beautiful lines.

> *We slowed again,*
> *And as the tightened brakes took hold, there swelled*
> *A sense of falling, like an arrow-shower*
> *Sent out of sight, somewhere becoming rain.*

A string of observations earlier in the poem abruptly becomes something more: a meditation on death, change, and the immutability of human nature, reflected in the vast, unchanging landscape of the train ride through Lincolnshire. This sweep up into vast timelessness from a run of quotidian detail completes a journey: the protagonist first sees only detail, but later realizes, through his observations on the old-fashioned rituals of Pentecostal weddings, the value of tradition and continuity. This is how Christianity works: from the mundane to the transcendent. But who will be able to read such poems in future, if the tradition on which they depend is overridden by social justice agendas—or Islam?

Pope Emeritus Benedict XVI, speaking in Paris in 2008, insisted that all the creativity of western civilization is grounded in God as maker, in whose image we are made, most particularly through the singing of the Psalms: "This intrinsic requirement of speaking with God and singing of him with words he himself has given, is what gave rise to the great tradition of Western music.

"It was not a form of private 'creativity,' in which the individual leaves a memorial to himself and makes self-representation his essential criterion. Rather it is about vigilantly recognizing with the 'ears of the heart' the inner laws of the music of creation, the archetypes of music that the Creator built into his world and into men, and thus discovering music that is worthy of God, and at the same time truly worthy of man, music whose worthiness resounds in purity."

This is why many of us, raised on Velázquez and Beethoven, find Islamic art and architecture so barren, and even sinister. Its endless, oppressive geometric regularity and blanket ban on faces and recognizable forms doesn't just forsake reaching for the divine: it forbids it. And the most emotionally expressive and spiritually uplifting medium of all, music, is expressly frowned upon and even explicitly banned.

Understanding the spiritual locus of western art's unique power to move us requires some understand-

ing of the Middle Ages.   Acquaint yourself with
Byzantine mosaics and Romanesque carvings and it
becomes clear to you why removing God from the creative process leaves you with the spiritual barrenness
of contemporary art.   And, understanding this, you
understand why the progressive Left is so desperate
to tear down anything transcendent or beautiful in
popular culture: because beauty leads back to God,
and God is a rival power center the cultural Marxists
cannot allow to survive.

VIII

SCHISM

Medieval Studies sits at the top of the academic mountain, like the Holy City of Jerusalem. It is the summit of scholarly enquiry into the beauty and mystery and majesty of European peoples and cultures, and the best set of tools the academy can offer to help us understand how the extraordinary accomplishments of western society came to be. It is the best explanation for the pre-eminence of the West and, of course, the richest defense of Christianity. If the corrupting rot of social justice sets in here and dissolves the integrity of the curriculum and body of knowledge in the academy, and it pollutes and overtakes Medieval Studies conferences, journals and departments, the humanities are truly doomed.

Successful resistance to social justice incursions is rare, but it has happened—and recently. The Gamergate controversy of 2014 saw video game enthusiasts tarred as abusers, harassers, and trolls, and baselessly accused of a bevy of horrendous things—all for the crime of demanding that their hobby should remain free from the pernicious influence of opportunistic but poorly-informed feminist critics and corrupt trade journalists. But the gamers won: gender warriors were left licking their wounds after failing to take over the gaming industry just as they had the worlds of comic books, fantasy fiction and sci-fi.

Several academics contacted thought Fulton Brown should focus on the surprising fact that she wasn't fired, which tells its own, monumentally depressing story. Adrian Johns, acting Chair of History at Chicago referred me to the department's previous statement and said he had nothing to add, while the usual Chair, Emilio Kourí, currently on leave, responded more briskly: "The Department does not intervene in academic disputes involving its members."

Jane Chance says that's not good enough. She notes the damage Fulton Brown's rabid critics have been attempting to inflict on her reputation and career prospects. "It's not just that Rachel has been hurt or is disappointed people have lied about her. Her career could be stymied because of all the letter-writing. It isn't fair. She is wounded from being attacked for being someone she is not. I would think that if the Chicago president believed in free speech and the University of Chicago really believed in free expression, they would support Rachel."

Chicago's position appears to be that it will not hinder Fulton Brown, as such, but it certainly will not help her. This is myopic. What has happened to Fulton Brown, and is currently unfolding in Medieval Studies, is the perfect microcosm of what is happening in academia at large, including Chicago's role in standing up for academic freedom. Just as Chicago is alone, so is Rachel Fulton Brown. How can the University of Chicago, rightly lauded for its attitude to academic freedom and freedom of speech, win the fight against trigger warnings and safe spaces if other universities don't recognize what it means to stand for academic freedom against the social justice warriors? Or for truth against social justice, as Jonathan Haidt puts it?

Nothing happening in Medieval Studies is new. The boycotts, petitions, demands for endless conference sessions about whiteness, activism in place of scholarship, social media mobs and the misuse of public money are the rule in many disciplines, especially subjects ending in "Studies." But unlike Gender Studies and Race Studies, Medieval Studies comes preloaded with a focus on a particular time and place, studied through different disciplinary modes.

If the gender and race warriors manage to dilute the Middle Ages into just another body of literature to be tossed into the social justice buzz-saw, it will obliterate the very thing that makes this field a field. If they are to survive the coming nuclear winter, humanities departments must rediscover a love of their own subjects, and reasons to read books again for their own sake and set aside activist agendas. No one else can provide the motivation to them—although Medieval Studies could provide a model for resistance, if it successfully repels the social justice invasion now.

"We are at the height of a wave of academic publishing shaming incidents that have terrified and intimidated an entire generation of scholars," says Landes. "You end up with senior people who say, 'I'm against boycotting Israel, but don't expect me to say that out loud because I don't want to damage my relationship with colleagues and students.' Scholars are not known for their courage, and in this case, we find a small but mobilized body who pick on those who don't strike back, bullying timid people who are afraid of public embarrassment and of the consequences for one's career."

A charitable interpretation of the wall of silence from Fulton Brown's side of this conflict, despite their greater numbers and the fact that the common-sense wing contains most, if not all, of the most well-respected figures in the field, would be that many academics are privately sympathetic, but too terrified to support Fulton Brown out loud, having seen what happens to colleagues who step outside the politically-correct consensus. But it is hard to view their reluctance to defend their own discipline as anything but self-serving cowardice—not to mention suicidal professional stupidity, given the vast body of evidence we now have about what happens to university departments and academic disciplines once they capitulate to the insatiable cult of social justice.

Until I began researching this story, only a small handful of her colleagues had come out in support of Rachel Fulton Brown, and most of them only privately. Among the many distinguished historians, authors and lecturers I spoke to, some of them for many hours over the telephone, only the few names you see here agreed to have their names included in the final copy. I am aware of only one letter sent to Fulton Brown's Dean in support. It was a private letter sent by one professor, and the author of that letter did not give me permission to quote from it or even identify him, fearing reprisals from the social justice wing of the field.

Astonishingly few academics are prepared to say in public what the rest of the country is thinking, but even tenured professors, at no risk of losing their jobs, are especially, inexplicably cowardly when it comes to defending one of their own, defending their own subject from vandals and, above all, defending the freedoms upon which their entire profession rests. Yet 1,500 scholars put their names to a letter based on a lie because the letter expressed the right politics. That speaks for itself.

For all their misguided ideas about race, and despite their ignorance of history, at least the alt-right appreciates the symbolic importance of the Middle Ages to the defense of western civilization—something Medieval Studies' own scholars seem to have set aside in favor of career safety. Academics who on the one hand explain to their students that serious inquiry into the Middle Ages has been the best route to European self-reflection have, on the other hand, done nothing to save their own field from convergence with destructive, self-indulgent victimhood narratives and Left-wing politics masquerading as scholarship.

The battle lines have already been drawn in this conflict, even if one side still stubbornly refuses to take up arms. No doubt many professors in Medieval Studies feel shame at their failure to resist, and their lack of courage when the time came to defend Rachel Fulton Brown from the couched-lance charge of false allegations. They are right to be ashamed. They can make amends by joining her on the front lines now.

Whether medieval historians can fight off the literature scholars determined to preoccupy their con-

ferences and academic journals with exhausting, pro-
tracted and useless hand-wringing about racism and
sexism depends on how seriously they take their own
statements about the position Medieval Studies commands in the academy and its significance as an academic endeavor. It will take vast reserves of courage
to shrug off zany allegations from the Left, and deft
social skills to avoid career disasters in the face of angry social justice mobs. But if the battle is not fought
and won now, there will be little left in a decade's time
to defend.

POSTSCRIPT

Rachel Fulton Brown remains a tenured professor at the University of Chicago. Many of her colleagues have apologized to her in the aftermath of Medieval-gate, pledging to take more care signing open letters in future. Following the publication of this essay, the National Association of Scholars organized an open letter in support of Fulton Brown, drawing attention to the slanders made by her critics. It attracted over a thousand signatures. The Medieval Academy has instituted a Professional Behavior Policy warning against "harassment" and "bullying." Matt Gabriele was attacked by Eileen Joy in April 2019 for a piece in the *Washington Post*, in which he looked forward to Notre Dame cathedral being rebuilt after a fire. She warned that the "theme of resurrection … is one of the core aspects of white supremacist appropriations." Joy herself is asking for donations on Twitter to keep her publishing house, Punctum Books, in business. Dorothy Kim is yet to publish any scholarship.

ABOUT THE AUTHOR

Milo Yiannopoulos is an award-winning journalist, a *New York Times*-bestselling author, an international political celebrity, a free speech martyr, a comedian, an accomplished entrepreneur, a hair icon, a penitent and, to the annoyance of his many enemies, an exceedingly happy person. He is the most censored, most lied-about man in the world, banned from stepping foot on entire continents for his unapologetic commitment to free expression. But he is also, somehow, one of the most sought-after speakers anywhere, invited by foreign governments, wealthy individuals and even the occasional courageous private company to share his unique blend of laughter and war. Milo lurches from improbable triumph to improbable triumph, loathed by establishment Left and Right alike. His first book, *Dangerous*, sold over 200,000 copies, despite never being reviewed in any major publication. Milo lives in New Jersey with his husband, John.

CPSIA information can be obtained
at www.ICGtesting.com
Printed in the USA
LVHW040211280519
619246LV00001B/7/P

9 789527 303559